For Wally

First US Edition
First published in Great Britain by Walker Books Ltd

Library of Congress Cataloging in Publication Data
Handford, Martin
Where's Waldo?
Summary: The reader follows Waldo as he hikes around
the world and must try to find h m in the illustrations
of some of the crowded places he visits.
1. Literary recreations.   [1. Literary recreations.
2. Voyages and travels—Fiction.   3.Humorous stories]
I. Title.
PZ7.H1918Wh   1987   [Fic]   87-2606
ISBN 0-316-34293-9

20 19 18 17

Printed and bound by L.E.G.O., Vicenza, Italy

WHERE'S WALDO?

MARTIN HANDFORD

Little, Brown and Company
Boston   Toronto   London

HI, FRIENDS!

MY NAME IS WALDO.
I'M JUST SETTING OFF ON A WORLD-
WIDE HIKE. YOU CAN COME TOO.
ALL YOU HAVE TO DO IS FIND ME,
WHEREVER I GO.

I'VE GOT ALL I NEED — WALKING
STICK, KETTLE, MALLET, CUP,
BACKPACK, SLEEPING BAG,
BINOCULARS, CAMERA, SNORKEL,
BELT, BAG AND SHOVEL.

WHEN I WAS IN TOWN TODAY I SAW
LOTS OF INTERESTING THINGS.
A WINDOW CLEANER EVEN DROPPED
A BUCKET ON A MAN'S HEAD.
OUCH!

Waldo

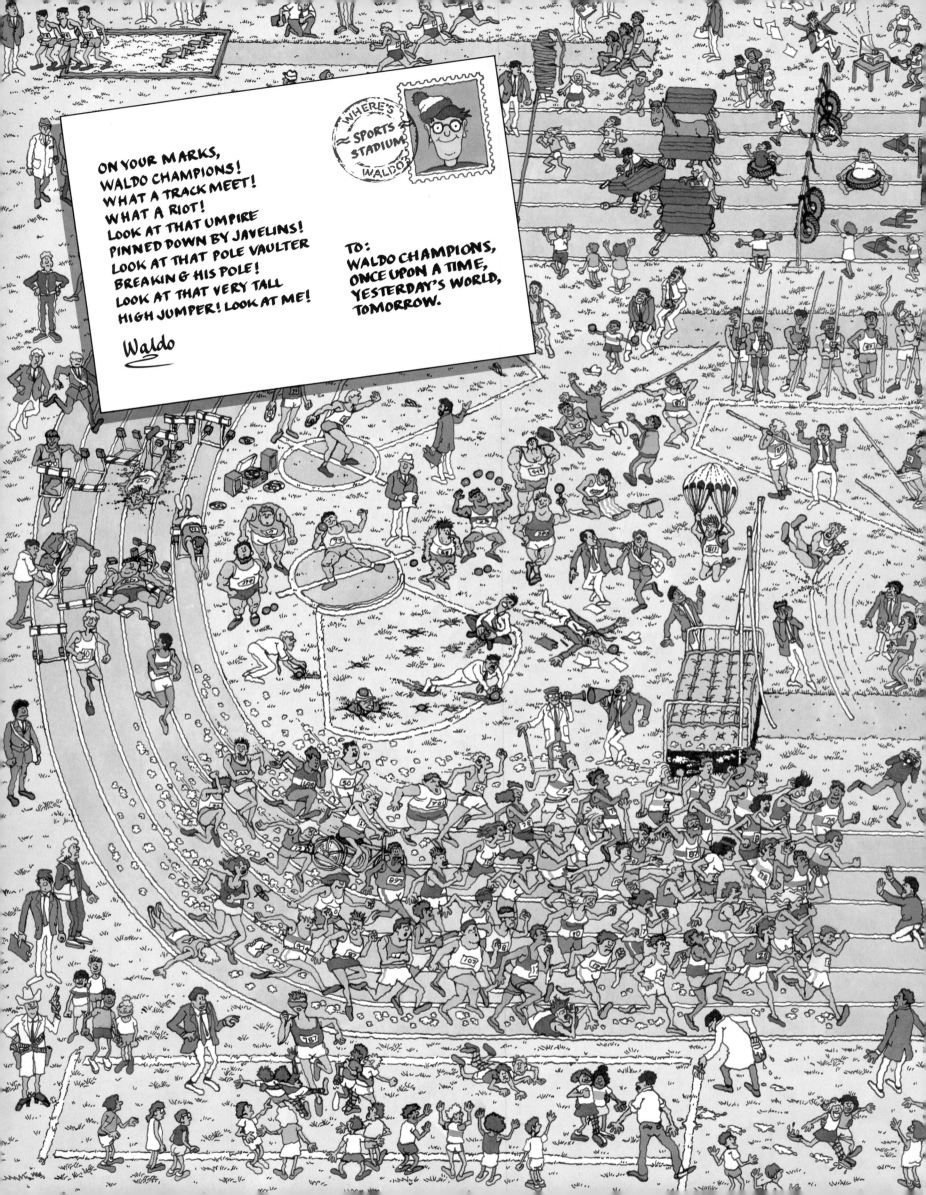

THE GREAT WHERE'S WALDO? CHECKLIST
Hundreds more things for Waldo watchers to watch out for!

IN TOWN
- A dog on a roof
- A man on a fountain
- A man about to trip over a dog's leash
- A car crash
- A keen barber
- People in a street, watching TV
- A puncture caused by a Roman arrow
- A tearful tune
- A boy attacked by a plant
- A waiter who isn't concentrating
- A robber who's been clobbered
- A face on a wall
- A man coming out of a manhole
- A man feeding pigeons
- A bicycle crash

SKI SLOPES
- A man reading on a roof
- A flying skier
- A runaway skier
- A backward skier
- A portrait in snow
- An illegal fisherman
- A snowball in the neck
- Two unconscious skiers
- Two skiers hitting trees
- An Alpine horn
- A snow skier
- A flag collector
- Two very scruffy skiers
- A skier up a tree
- A water skier on snow
- A Yeti
- A skiing reindeer
- A roof jumper
- A heap of skaters

THE RAILWAY STATION
- A boy falling from a train
- A breakdown on tracks
- Naughty children on a train roof
- People being knocked over by a door
- A man about to step on a ball
- Three different times at the same time
- A wheelbarrow baby carriage
- A face on a train
- Five people reading one newspaper
- A struggling bag carrier
- A show-off with suitcases
- A man losing everything from his cases
- A smoking train
- A squeeze on a bench
- A dog tearing a man's trousers
- Fare dodgers
- A hand caught between doors
- A cattle stampede
- A man breaking a weighing machine

ON THE BEACH
- A dog biting a boy's bottom
- A man who is overdressed
- A muscular man with a medal
- A popular girl
- A water skier on water
- A striped photo
- A punctured pontoon
- A donkey who likes ice cream
- A man being squashed
- A punctured beach ball
- A human pyramid
- A human stepping-stone
- Two odd friends
- A cowboy
- A human donkey
- Age and beauty
- A boy who follows in his father's footsteps
- Two men with undershirts, one without
- A boy being tortured by a spider
- A show-off with sandcastles
- A gang of hat robbers
- An Arab making pyramids
- Three protruding tongues
- Two oddly fitting hats
- An odd couple
- Five sprinters
- A towel with a hole in it
- A cactus
- A boy who's not allowed any ice cream

CAMP SITE
- A bull in a hedge
- Bull horns
- A shark in a canal
- A bull seeing red
- A careless kick
- Tea in a lap
- A low bridge
- People knocked over by a mallet
- A man surprised undressing
- A bicycle tire about to be punctured
- Camper's camels
- A scarecrow that doesn't work
- A wigwam
- Large biceps
- A collapsed tent
- A smoking barbecue
- A fisherman catching old boots
- Tacks on the path
- Boy scouts making fire
- A tired Santa
- A man blowing up a boat
- A camper's butler
- Runners on a road
- A bull chasing children
- Scruffy campers
- Thirsty walkers

SPORTS STADIUM
- Three pairs of feet, sticking out of sand
- A cowboy starting races
- Hopeless hurdlers
- Ten children with fifteen legs
- A record thrower
- A shot-put juggler
- An ear trumpet
- A vaulting horse
- A racer with two wheels
- A parachuting vaulter
- A Scotsman with a caber
- An elephant pulling a rope
- People being knocked over by a hammer
- A gardener
- Three frogmen
- A naked runner
- A bed
- A bandaged boy
- A runner with four legs
- A sunken jumper
- A man with an odd pair of legs
- A man chasing a dog, chasing a cat
- A boy squirting water